# POETIC INJUSTICE:
## A RHYME CRIME

*To Bonnie & Grady*
*with some good wishes*

By George Statham

*George E. Statham*

Library of Congress Catalog Card Number: 95-90809

ISBN 1-57502-165-X

Fireside Publishing, PO Box 282, Hiawassee, GA 30546

*Additional copies are available. For your convenience, an order form can be found at the back of this book.*

Printed in the USA by Morris Publishing. 3212 E. Hwy 30, Kearney, NE 68847. 800-650-7888

*This book came about after writing poems about myself, family, friends, and my varied experiences in the outdoor life, having spent many hours in the woods and Boy Scout camps with my troop, BSA Troop 79, Carbon Hill, Alabama.*

*My memory of life on the primitive farm in rural North Texas gave me a lot of thought and material to consider in all my writing. Life on the farm was hard work, good eating, and a healthy life, but we didn't know it.*

*I don't see how you can write about us in the South unless you consider the American political scene. We have to either poke fun at it or sit down and cry. I have considered some things seriously, as in this life, indeed, we must.*

*This work came about after my son, Robert Statham, asked for a copy of what I had written.*

*Please don't take it too seriously.*

*I am grateful for the patient work and assistance given by my son, Ross Statham, in the layout, design, and many hours of patient counseling reviewing the manuscript and, of course, in his efficient typesetting of all of it.*

*GES*

# POETIC INJUSTICE:
## A RHYME CRIME

## Table of Contents

# BISCUIT BREAD

I love biscuits by the pan
A real treat for any man.
Served up hot with real butter,
Can eat 'em fast and never stutter.

They are good when on the table
Are homemade, don't have a label.
Many girls make by hand
Others would simply open a can.

When you do it, bake 'em brown
You're soon too fat to get around.
Some folks think they have been fed
With a piece of plain light bread.

A biscuit is a favorite food
To pass 'em up would be rude.
Please look up when brother passes,
He is reachin' for the 'lasses.

———◆———

*If you don't like the Deep South it's just a
matter that you ain't got deep enough.*

# MULASSES

We have syrup and blackstrap,
Good enough for me and Pap.
Blackstrap is our Southern 'lasses
Now I can eat all they passes.

Grow 'em out on our land,
Cut and gathered all by hand.
Now we haul it to the mill,
Me and Dad and James and Bill.

None of us are not a fool,
But the mill is run by mule.
Now he cannot work the fastest,
Guess he made some real mulasses.

———◆———

*Down South, "dassent" simply means you
better not do it– and you better not*

# CLABBER

Buttermilk and cornbread,
Eat it 'fore I go to bed.
When I have a growin' yearn
I simply go and check the churn.

We don't make it every day,
Still is none to throw away.
If you're slow and do not grabber,
May end up with just some clabber.

Way down South we have clabber,
All the folks will try to nab 'er.
If you want a little more,
You won't find it in the store.

———◆———

*Have already started writing another book of
verse, but this one is just for the pun of it.*

# PEACH CLOBBER

Down South we have peach clobber,
Dull fish hooks, and a bobber.
My wife bakes it with a crust,
Another bowl and I will bust.

Peaches grown on any farm,
Eatin' them will cause no harm.
Like to pull 'em off the tree,
On my place they all are free.

I pray a little and make speeches,
But I like them Georgia peaches.
With a crust all golden brown,
Ain't no trouble a gettin' down.

———◆———

*I applied for a poetic license, but it ain't come through yet.*

# SWEETNIN'

Folks down South of all classes
Live on bread and real molasses.
Biscuit bread is what they eat,
But a little 'lasses makes it sweet.

You can eat it when you're fed,
It also goes with our cornbread.
Have a snack at mid-night,
Spread a biscuit at first light.

I have et it fifty years,
When wife can't get she sheds tears.
Now we hope her bad mood passes,
I will go and get some 'lasses.

———◆———

*If a preacher don't preach to beat the devil*
*what is he preachin' for?*

# HOG KILLIN'

Hog meat and greens is where it's at,
Consume before you're old and fat.
Now I grew up on a farm,
It actually did me little harm.

Me and Pa, we killed the hogs,
Saved a little for the dogs.
Renderin' lard and curin' ham
We didn't pay our Uncle Sam.

Work was hard, the ground was rough,
In fifty years we had enough.
I know I'm old and half unstable,
But she don't help me to the table.

———◆———

*Trade - pork bellies;*
*boil - sow bellies;*
*but it ain't good for all bellies.*

# CHICORY COFFEE

Chicory coffee from the South,
Drink it hot in my mouth.
I can drink it day or night.
Some have said I ain't real bright.

Many throw out and make waste
Cause they haven't got the taste.
Now I tell you I ain't wrong,
That is mud that's really strong.

Way up North it ain't found,
But down South we look around.
Sent my wife and Cousin Fran
For a pack of Luzianne.

———◆———

*Jumbaliar is only a dishonest Cajun*

# CORNPONE

Way down South we eat cornbread,
Hope to eat it til I'm dead.
With turnip greens and buttermilk,
Slides on down as smooth as silk.

We have hog meat and hominy grits,
Keeps us Southerns from havin' fits.
Spare ribs baked right in the pan
And a sweet tater for the man.

Country ham and red eye gravy,
Good enough for the U.S. Navy.
Buttermilk biscuits in a plate,
I am good for seven or eight.

Corn bread and biscuits for all classes
Goes real good with Southern 'lasses.
If you think my sayin' rude
You must go try our Southern food.

———◆———

*Bill said, "I have committed another culinary
indiscretion," but all it was he had just et too
much.*

# CHICKENS

Way down South we like chicken,
It don't have to be finger lickin'.
Please don't think it is depressin',
Many times he's baked with dressin'.

Sometimes boil 'em in the pot,
We all like it warm or hot.
Dumplins are dropped in the pan,
We can eat 'em, man oh man.

Now don't get mad or take offense,
I have pulled them off the fence.
Chickens are loud and plenty dumb,
Still I think I must have some.

Killed two roosters for my bride,
Now she made 'em Southern fried.
It don't matter how you feel,
Will make us both a real good meal.

# CRACKLINS

My boys are healthy, they've been fed.
They grew up on cracklin' bread.
Butchered hogs behind the barn,
Shot 'em dead, we didn't warn.

Boiled sow-belly in a pot,
And that is all the lard we got.
Poured the lard up in a can,
Cracklins given to each man.

Cracklins are a Southern tradition,
But it ain't called good nutrition.
We keep on eatin', we've been fed,
Now you guessed it, in cornbread.

———————◆———————

*To tell you the truth, clabber is just milk
goin' AWOL.*

# LARD

Saturated fat is bad for our health,
Short or fat or with wealth.
In the South we eat hog meat,
And we like our taters sweet.

Too much fat will give us trouble,
Cause your girth to go and double.
We like our grub Southern fried,
Grandad et it til he died.

We been told to quit fat eatin',
It's as bad as too much sweeten,
Will keep a workin' til I drop,
But I must have a fat pork chop.

———◆———

*One thing I gotta say about my new diet,*
*"There ain't nothin' to it."*

11

# TURNIP GREENS

Turnip greens and sow belly,
Good enough for Doyle and Nellie.
Ain't afraid of gettin' sicker
Cause I had my own pot liquor.

All boiled up in a pot,
We were glad for what we got.
Ham goes good with the above,
Cause it's what we really love.

You pull the greens and turnips, too,
We can't get by with just a few.
I have et 'em all my life,
Same is said by my dear wife.

◆

*Worse verse is what I seem to do a lot of.*

# JAVA

I like coffee in a pot,
But it must be pipin' hot.
Have it in my fishin' camp
Will go drink it, dry or damp.

Build you up a fire of wood,
That will make it pretty good.
Get your water from the creek,
But be sure it isn't weak.

Get a goin' at first light,
Coffee helps me lose the night.
Can do allright when I am up
If and when she brings a cup.

———◆———

*Sure, I still chase women, but nowadays I just walk.*

# CORN

Corn was planted near the creek,
Finished up way last week.
Mules are willin' to drag the plow,
A real good crop will feed the sow.

Corn is good for feedin' men,
Some have got to drink it in.
Seen a lot of men get sicker
All because of their corn liquor.

It is food for men and hogs,
Give a little to the dogs.
Wife she boils it on the cob,
Thinks it is an easy job.

I have et it all my life,
We can cook it, me and wife.
Now we had it again today,
Wasn't none to throw away.

# A SOUTHERN STORY

I tell tales of the South
When I ain't down in the mouth.
Don't drink likker and never smoke,
My next door neighbor was a soak.

Love the South and it's stories,
Civil War and it's glories.
Great Grandad was in the fight,
He was burnt out late one night.

You've heard my tale, it is a fact,
Only had the clothes on his back.
This here story ain't a sin,
Cause the South will rise agin.

———◆———

*Don't worry, trouble will always blow over -
on you, of course.*

# SICKNESS

Have a case of bad colitis,
Also down with my nephritis,
And my heart is plumb unsteady;
If it gives out I ain't ready.

Lost my teeth to gingivitis
Then bacteria came to fight us.
Cataracts and failin' sight
Barely get me thru the night.

Joints and back are worn out,
Also comin' down with gout.
Sure am glad that I ain't broke,
Think I'm fixin' to have a stroke.

I am old and have some wear,
But there is still my Medicare.
Guv'ment says they will give aid,
But most of us are still afraid.

# HOGS

Pigs are pigs, but I like hogs,
Also wimmen and old hound dogs.
I tell the truth, I ain't a funnin'
Even when the bull is runnin'.

Down in the South we have class,
Good lookin' wimmen and bigmouth bass.
Bass are great when they are swimmin',
But my choice is still the wimmen.

Hogs are kept out in a pen,
Fed and slopped by us men.
The dogs are bred for common good.
We all like 'em and hope you would.

Can't say more about the wimmen,
Some are fat and need a slimmin'.
Whatever you choose for a wife,
Please remember it's for life.

# WALLEYED

Said to my wife, do not sass,
I am goin' to catch a bass.
Now she said it's way too late
And besides there is no bait.

We talked it over quite a bit,
Then she had a walleyed fit.
Can't go fishin' you ol nut,
Wait til after the yard is cut.

Cut the grass a little faster
Cause I am still the lord and master.
She finally said go on out,
Can't catch fish beyond a doubt.

Went a stalkin' thru the grass,
Caught a trout and one sandbass.
Couldn't bring fish home to maw,
Cause they had taken the lockjaw.

# DRAGGIN'

Go to the mountains to cut wood,
Think I'm gettin' pretty good.
Cut a big oak just last week,
But I dropped it in the creek.

Couldn't get it worked all day,
But I watched it float away.
A woodsman's what I hope to be,
The work is hard as you can see.

Keep a cuttin' and draggin' logs,
Me and the truck and two of the dogs.
I think I should drop the logs,
And go ahead and drag the dogs.

———◆———

*Have seen lots of huntin' dogs - from hounds,
pointers, and setters. All of mine have only
been petters.*

# THE MINER

Diggin' up coal ain't cause it's funny,
The usual interest is simply money.
Tunnel way down and blast it loose,
In any event it's put to use.

Some people scrape back a little soil,
A whole lot better than drillin' oil.
Then scoop it up and haul it away,
The more they haul, the more they pay.

There's extra hard work there in the pits,
But a bloomin' coal miner is paid for it.
Now the U M W and the C I and O,
That ol boy brings home the dough.

In times way back in a company shack
They did their best to break his back.
He went down early and came up late,
Was hard on him as well as his mate.

The pay is good, the work is bad,
I aim to keep diggin' just like Dad.
This fellow down the road he got hung,
But I'll hold out for my Black Lung.

# GARDENIN'

Put a garden in the yard,
Found the diggin' really hard.
We simply had to have some maters,
But no room for the pertaters.

Put out peppers and cauliflower,
It was done in half an hour.
Then put onions in the ground,
And leaf lettuce all around.

The garden growed and got bigger,
Rabbit felt the pull of trigger.
We saw a squirrel a passin' by,
Was pretty sure that he would die.

Growin' a garden, it ain't hard.
Hate the diggin' in the yard.
Wife she loves me - will not grovel,
But she makes me use the shovel.

# ELLIRIDGE

I've lived in Georgia over a year,
We have catfish, trout, and deer.
In the mountains, near the creek,
It's what I like, I ain't a freak.

Several towns are nearby,
Real estate is extra high.
Guess I won't buy in that town,
Have to make the price come down.

I took a drive the other day
Then I went to Ellijay.
Now Blue Ridge was enroute,
It was small, but it was cute.

We looked all over at each town
And we liked what we had found.
Looked around for over a day,
Would be Elliridge or Blue Jay.

# THE LEADER

Dear ol Dad ain't gettin' faster,
But he is our best scoutmaster.
He signed up to teach the boys,
Poor cooked meals and plenty noise.

Out to the woods and pitch a tent,
Sixteen boys, they packed and went.
Pitched their camp right on the creek,
Had only two days, but wanted a week.

All day long they did their lookin',
Caught some fish and did the cookin'.
Outdoor life is extra sweet,
But Boy Scout cookin' I can't eat.

Brought 'em together at end of day
To all go home - we knew the way.
Packed the truck and loaded gear,
But soap and water they won't get near.

# MOUNTAIN LIFE

Think I have a pretty good life,
On the mountain with my wife.
She keeps the house, bakes the bread,
Tell you now we both are fed.

She takes to the river, me and canoe,
Picks me up when I am thru.
Last time out it was faster,
Cause I had a boat disaster.

I upset in the creek,
Will do it again this comin' week.
All my tackle went downstream,
That's a fact and not a dream.

Caught the boat 'tho soakin' wet,
That is the 15th canoe upset.
Like to ride on down the stream
So I can look and fish and dream.

# MUSIC

If you think my verse is wrong,
I may put it in a song.
Really like it quite a liddle
Even when I play the fiddle.

Told you stories, various rhymes,
But never yet of no crimes.
Of dogs and wimmen and floatin' a boat,
But never one of a billy goat.

Can't set verses to a tune,
Cause my music is immune.
Can read music and write verse,
All agree the latter's worse.


# LOVE

Wimmen are what we really need,
When you love one, is no greed.
Fell in love with quite a few,
But I got one all brand new.

We got married way down South,
Then I bussed her on the mouth.
I liked that an awful lot,
Was in love with what I got.

# MOUNTAIN BIRDS

Ruffed grouse, a mountain bird,
I have seen and I have heard.
Hunt 'em on the mountain steep,
Down a loggin' road I must creep.

He is small and he is sly,
Willin' to let you walk on by.
If you stop and look around,
In a while he leaves the ground.

Thunders up and thru the trees,
Makes you weak in both knees.
Unlock your gun and make a shot,
Now them birds are hardly got.


# VENISON

Hunted deer way out West,
But the eatin' I liked best.
Venison roasted with a tater,
If you try will not hate 'er.

Deer looked up with soleful eyes,
Couldn't shoot, I realize.
Guess I am a real disgrace,
Cause he stopped and made a face.

# MY DOG

Now my mutt is a valuable dog,
Lay in your lap and snore like a hog,
Sleep all day and most of the night,
Won't chase a cat or start a fight.

A good watch dog, she cannot be,
Sleepin' all time, she cannot see.
Can guard the house and all the yard,
The way she does it isn't hard.

Won't tree a cat or chase a squirrel,
This little mutt is a priceless pearl.
She'll go to sleep in a Boy Scout Camp,
Wet or dry or even damp.

She's been down river in my boat,
Perfect dog on a Southern float.
A real companion who's willin' to nap,
Sit in the boat with her in my lap.

# UPSET

I am old and kind of weak
I upset while in the creek.
In the water floatin' a boat,
It was serene and real remote.

Put me in up near the park,
Promised to be home after dark.
Caught two trout in some pools,
Also passed two fishin' fools.

I was floatin', doin' great,
Fish a snappin' at the bait.
Took the rapids round the bend,
I upset; that is the end.


# VOTIN'

Was goin' to town for to vote,
But I got the urge to float.
So I went out on the creek,
Vote it absent this comin' week.

Wife, she thought I was wise,
And not like the other guys.
I ain't scared about the votin',
But I have to go a floatin'.

# GEORGIA

Georgia is a wonderful state,
We don't think it second rate.
I came here from Arkansas,
And we liked all we saw.

In the mountains, near the creeks,
Have been fishin' for several weeks.
Brasstown Bald is nearby,
Here in Geogia that is high.

Moved to the country, but near town,
While still able to get around.
Have been in the city; it's the pits,
Congested drivin' gives me fits.

———◆———

*I got so mad at meetin' the other night I hit
the guy right in the fist with my nose.*

# SPOT

My dog Spot has it made,
All he does is lay in the shade.
Just a dog, we like him fine.
Still and all he is mine.

I have had him several years,
Points trout and chases deers.
He don't talk or ever brag,
But his tail can really wag.

He ain't pretty and isn't fair,
To tell the truth, he doesn't care.
He's got some age and showin' wear;
Will put him in for Peticare.

———◆———

*Someone said years ago, "Time wounds all heels."*

# SOLID ROCK

Of all the rock groups I have heard
There ain't any like no kind of bird.
Heard the Beetles and Fifth Dimension,
More serenity in a political convention.

I know I'm gettin' old and cannot stand,
This intense racket shakin' the land.
I love good music played on guitar,
What they are doin' would wreck a car.

The Jefferson Airplane was called real
   good,
Can't agree, but was sure you would.
Things do change, especially with age,
The kids agree this is the rage.

Now solid rock it has it's thing,
But so did Bob and dear ol Bing.
I'm willin' to say before I'm sick,
Don't go for rock, just use a brick.

# DAD

Farmin' was my dad's perfession,
In 1930 during Depression.
Lost his job and his car,
It was worse than in the war.

Had a wife, would not forsake 'er,
Helped him work up ever acre.
By workin' hard and cuttin' wood
They finally got it pretty good.

They canned corn and put up peas,
In those days no deep freeze.
Growed terbaccer on the hill,
Escaped a payin' that one bill.

He loved the farm and he was willin',
Was pretty good at hog killin'.
Now we boys thought it rotten
When we had to pick the cotton.

# COTTON

Cotton is a Southern crop,
I don't grow it, had to stop.
Grandad planted in the ground,
Had no time to go to town.

You must plow, then you chop,
If it rains may get a crop.
Walk along behind a mule,
Sure is hot; it ain't cool.

A crop is good, it ain't evil,
There is still the ol boll weevil.
Now I ain't workin' in the field,
The city had a higher yield.

———◆———

*Preacher said as he pulled the kid from the
creek, "Tell me, little man, how did you come
to fall in?" The kid replied, "I didn't come to
fall in; I came to fish."*

# COTTON PICKIN'

Workin' the farm is gettin' slicker
Now they have a cotton picker.
We bent over and drug a sack,
Bout enough to break your back.

You drug the sack a full day,
Real hard work and little pay.
Stayed at home, we had no tents,
And we were glad for fifty cents.

Went to town at the end of the week,
A little fun we had to seek.
We pulled the cotton from early morn,
Now why not drink a little corn.

———◆———

*Wife said, "Oh, I lost eight pounds." I
answered, "Wherbouts?" Ain't no way you
can please a woman.*

# CATS

My kid loves cats, the domestic kind.
She even thinks they are extra fine.
Of all the animals I have found,
I give my vote to the dear ol hound.

Now I ain't one to be upset
Over your own choice of a pet.
A cat may be fine as a bobwhite quail,
But he sure won't ever wag his tail.

From alley cat to pure manx,
I ain't gonna offer any thanks.
Of all the animals I have met,
A faithful dog is the only pet.

———◆———

*My sayin's are dum...try 'em some.*

# SHOOTIN'

I went huntin' for to shoot a quail,
My faithful dog, he hit the trail.
He pointed a bird, I took a shot,
The cleanest miss I ever got.

Went a little further walkin' straight,
My gun was loaded with number eight.
He found the birds up near the trees.
Cocked my gun and strengthened my
    knees.

Now one flew up and then another,
My automatic blowed away the cover.
Emptied the gun of all its load,
But I got one walkin' up the road.

Now shootin' at birds is my delight,
Caused me and my wife to have a fight.
I don't worry about my mate,
My shootin' may cause the dog to hate.

# DATIN'

Southern girls are extra sweet
If not too fat or indiscreet.
My friend got one way too funny,
Still and all it was his honey.

You look 'em over and make a date,
Many times she will be late.
It don't matter 'bout the time
Cause bein' late is not a crime.

If you want to get a gurl,
You must culture like a pearl.
We wish a lot and wonder why,
Without a gal we can't get by.

———◆———

*It has been determined that a fat girl is just a
young lardy.*

37

# GIRLS

I like girls of all classes,
Dearly love those Southern lasses.
Got me one forty years ago,
And I ain't fixin' to let go.

Girls are girls and lasses are lasses,
Are more fun than eight pound basses.
One is enough for any man,
But not the custom of the land.

Love these girls here in the South,
Like to kiss 'em on the mouth.
Whatever you think of these classes,
We have got to have mo' lasses.

———◆———

*Hard work is difficult to get acquainted with.*

## DOG RUNNIN'

Drinkin' likker and runnin' dogs,
And fallin' off a slippery log.
Out in the woods under the moon,
Thirteen men a runnin' a coon.

That don't sound like too much fun,
But you don't have to bring a gun.
Hound dog music beneath the stars,
Better than bein' up on Mars.

Now we all did it the other night,
Hound dogs had an awful fight.
It's a bad habit, can't excuse it.
Still we have to go and dooze it.


## BOAT DOG

Dog crawled in with me and boat,
I could see he wanted to float.
Pushed it out into the stream,
It was a fact and not a dream.

Floated boat, both me and dog,
Almost hung up on a log.
Hated to do it to ol Rover,
But I went and turned it over.

# DOGS

Huntin' dogs, we all had
Two for maw and six for dad.
Had to go and chase a coon,
Heard 'em talkin' to the moon.

Runnin' dogs late at night
Was me and brother's real delight.
Treed the coon high in an oak,
With the rifle we would croak.

Huntin' late til early morn,
Caused us late to plant the corn.
Corn is better than a thistle
Cause it helps us wet our whistle.


# CUSSIN' DOG

Shootin' birds is more than fun.
You don't shoot 'em on the run.
Have to shoot a flyin' bird,
On the ground, it is unheard.

Take my dog and blunderbuss,
Didn't know that dog could cuss.
He had seen me shoot before,
I don't think he wanted more.

# CORN LIKKER

I've seen 'em old, I've seen 'em frisky,
Seen the fools a drinkin' whiskey.
Many men will scream and shout,
Cause they cannot do without.

Much corn likker made down South,
Ain't gonna put it in my mouth.
You drink it and you think you're smart,
Then your reason will depart.

I tried it many years ago,
Tell you boys I have let go.
If you get over your achin' head,
May finally feel you ain't dead.

———◆———

*The NRA is gunnin' for all of us!*

# HOMEBREW

We made homebrew in the cellar,
Made enough for every feller.
Grandpa used a great big crock;
Run the liquid through his sock.

We let it work about a week,
Bottles and capper we did seek.
Bottled up and put away
We could drink it every day.

Homebrew is a pretty good drink.
It don't matter what you think.
Some don't like a little bit,
So all you have to do is quit.

———◆———

*A lot of public speakers deliver three times
more to the front end than the back end can
endure.*

# OUT WEST

Out in Texas it don't rain,
I have seen it again and again.
When you try to get a crop,
Is no water, not a drop.

Planted early with Spring rain,
Might as well have gone to Maine.
Cloud came up but not a drop,
But if it starts, will not stop.

Farmin' the West is takin' a chance,
More than likely lose your pants.
Neighbor told me what I oughter,
So I got some dried out water.

———◆———

*Told my wife she got a real good man when
she got married. She said, "That's strange, I
thought I married you."*

# A CRACKER

This is about a Georgia Cracker,
Grows and chews his own terbaccer.
Chewin' terbaccer is his need,
He will have it after he feeds.

In a plug or even twist,
He will cram it in his fist.
He may stop and shoot a rabbit,
Simply cannot stop the habit.

His wife has called it real unclean,
Of this habit she can't wean.
Hope she doesn't have a fit,
Cause he will only stop and spit.

———◆———

*As the boxer said after the TKO, "I have
never seen better daze."*

# GROUSE SHOOTIN'

Shootin' at grouse is really fun,
I ain't ever come close to one.
I have missed 'em flying away,
Shot two boxes the other day.

Hear 'em drummin' on a log,
It excites both me and dog.
Dog comes along, will not point.
Guess his nose is out of joint.

Walk the trails by the creek,
Hunt and shoot about a week.
Flies up fast without a sound,
My blunderbuss will bring him down.

Bring it home for her to pluck,
She wishes I had had no luck.
Set it in a roastin' pan,
Was all et up by her and man.

# HUNTIN'

Huntin' is a lot of fun,
It ain't approved by everyone.
We get support from the NRA
Who always have a lot to say.

But shootin' is the American way,
Cannot stop it whatever you say.
Grandpa kept his gun on the hill,
How else can you look after a workin'
    still?

We love to hunt deer and bear in the hills,
It don't matter you can't pay the bills.
With the ducks goin' South and geese
    flyin' by,
Your wife just wonders, she don't know
    why.

## OL MUTT

Now ol Spot up and died,
Grandma wept and really cried.
Had been with us quite a spell,
We could both see he wasn't well.

Took to the vet just last week,
Said,"That ol mutt is up the creek.
He is old and gettin' thin,
I am sure he's near the end."

Spot passed on the next day.
We were sad as he went away.
Makes me sad and I grieve,
Sure did hate to see him leave.


## QUAIL

Shootin' quail, a great pastime,
My performance is a crime.
I can shoot and do not cuss,
Have a real good blunderbuss.

Point a covey, took a bead,
But I gave him too much lead.
The bird flew on across the creek,
If not today, there is next week.

# FIDDLE SONG

I have writ a fiddle song,
It was flat and way too long.
Sounded a great deal like a loon.
Maybe it was out of tune.

I write the notes; ain't the best,
Forgot to have a sixteenth rest.
2-4 time is for the fiddle
Even if you play but liddle.

I did practice plenty long,
Ain't no doubt, a real bad song.
Neighbors came to hear me play
Both they and dogs, they ran away.

———◆———

*High conceit will bring defeat.*

# MY FIDDLE

Took my fiddle from the case,
Wife, she took a can of mace.
She had heard me play before.
And said can't take no more.

Took my fiddle to the cellar,
To tell the truth I was yeller.
Played a tune up thru the vent,
Then the cellar door was rent.

Now ol Spot was walkin' by,
Didn't know that he could cry.
Cat left home with a sack,
And he said ain't comin' back.

———◆———

*I have made a liddle playing the fiddle. Wife
said, "I'll give you three bucks if you will put
that up."*

# TO TEXAS

Went to Texas the other day,
Wife, she drove about half way.
It was pleasant without dissent,
But we had an argument.

Road signs bad - map is wrong.
I have told you all along.
You're drivin' too fast and wastin' gas,
If we get there, will be last.

Talked it over a day or two,
She got done and she was thru.
But to keep from bein' late,
We got on the Interstate.

———◆———

*Have you heard the story about the destitute
rattlesnake? He didn't have a pit to hiss in.*

# RAINFALL

Rained in the mountains late last week.
All the water ran out of the creek.
Rained two days and half the night.
Gave me and Grandma a terrible fright.

It was so much we couldn't get out,
To see the neighbors, had to shout.
It let up at break of day.
We were glad when it went away.

Raindrops drop from a cloud;
May be soft or may be loud.
In case my story is in doubt,
Our lightnin' bugs have shorted out.

————◆————

*Ignorance gone to seed usually germinates
into trouble.*

# COONS

Treein' coons is allright,
It all happens in the night.
Hope the story don't confound,
You must have a treein' hound.

We had eight dogs runnin' round,
Through the woods and over the ground.
We had to run and then to walk
Listenin' to them hound dogs talk.

We got home before first light,
Dogs had run us all the night.
I am tired and hungry, too,
Now it's all over, I am thru.


# TURKEY HUNTIN'

I hunt turkey in Tennessee,
But no bird will come to me.
Take my caller and I squawk,
But I ain't heard no turkey talk.

Set under a tree in a camo suit,
Ain't seen nuthin I can shoot.
Used my caller half a day,
Guess that gobbler walked away.

# OL SPOT

Dear ol Spot is just a dog,
Most as lazy as a hog.
Will be my dog to the end,
He's truly been my best friend.

All the family like him some,
He's old and slow, not really dum.
Used to go and hunt with me,
Now it's hard to smell and see.

Spot has earned a place to rest,
When he was doin', gave his best.
Now he's layin' by the fire,
Just like me, he did retire.

———◆———

*You have to realize my tales about ol Spot are
about a generic dog.*

# A TUNE

I have told you all along
I am fixin' to write a song.
Think the tune must be neat,
Music cannot be incomplete.

Can get the words, not the notes,
Even when my wife-mate quotes.
Put it up in 2-4 time.
It was sweet and had a rhyme.

Played it on my country fiddle,
And it broke it in the middle.
Wife had heard me stop and play,
She promptly said, "Go throw away."

———◆———

*Many of us have been worried for years about
ethics in government. You really shouldn't
worry since there ain't any.*

# IN THE MOUNTAINS

Lived in the mountains several years
Play with grouse and trout and deers.
It has beauty, it is sublime,
If you ain't afraid to climb.

Up on the mountain, it is neat
At about four thousand feet.
Build a cabin on the top
After we get the tree to drop.

Many logs went to the mill,
Lumber came back up the hill.
Built it solid out of spruce,
Nailed up tight by me and Bruce.

The cabin built, we did it well,
But now we have to go and sell.
Advertised it in the press,
But only made another mess.

# VERSE WRITIN'

Sit at home a writin' verse.
They are gettin' worse and worse.
I don't think it is a crime,
But it is a good pastime.

Stories of fish, wimmen, and water,
Even one about my dotter.
Hound dogs runnin' round the place,
Guess I'll be a real disgrace.

I am old, my back is bent,
Still I get encouragement.
Even tho my arm is sore,
I am goin' to write some more.


# FAR AWAY

Over the hill and far away
Was a song I wrote today.
Fiddle a tune all night long,
That ol man can ruin a song.

Over the hill has one more verse,
Can't really tell which is worse.
May bury it on the lone prairie,
Just as long as the funeral's free.

# THE SKILLET

I love to drop a catfish fillet
Right down in a cast iron skillet.
Fried up brown they're really fetchin',
Still not as good as the catchin'.

Catfish is a Southern thing.
Makes us rednecks dance and sing.
Have caught up with quite a few,
Still don't eat catfish stew.

Went fishin' with my cousin.
We both caught an even dozen.
Now twenty-four catfish up and died,
That ain't bad cause they were fried.


# RABBITS

Huntin' rabbits in the yard,
Shoot 'em dead, it ain't hard.
He hopped into my garden,
That's a sin I will not pardon.

When I shoot they are dead.
And the rabbit gets us fed.
Guess it is a real bad habit,
But that's the end of Mr. Rabbit.

# SELLIN'

Went to sell my mountain land,
Ad in the paper, it was grand.
Many came to look around,
Up the mountain and over the ground.

Many looked and turned away,
Others wanted, but couldn't pay.
Price was right, terms were fair,
You deal with lots of real hot air.

I was tired, I was irate,
Wanted to sell that real estate.
Called a realtor to the land,
Thought it pretty, it was grand.

Had a contract in his car,
Said to sign it right down thar.
Signed the paper a year ago,
Tell you now, the sellin' slow.

# JAWS

Jaws are somethin' that have to flap,
Usually associated with a sap.
The female one is called the worst,
But please recall the man was first.

They always come in an even pair,
A perfect exit for pure hot air.
The ideal spot to place your grub,
But eatin' too fast may make a nub.

Teeth are usually found therein,
Thirty-two for full grown men.
They don't all come 'til you are grown,
The wisdom ones can make you moan.

The mandible is the lower thing,
It opens wide whenever you sing.
When opened wide to make a query,
It's all hooked up to the maxillary.

Jaws are located in the mouth.
One is north, the other is south.
I'm here to say that like a knife,
The dangerous one is on the wife.

# MININ'

Panning for gold on Coker Creek,
Broke my back in less than a week.
We sifted the gravel and a lot of sand,
But all we got was a worn out hand.

A sluice box is a better trap,
Your wife will shovel while you nap.
If both are lucky and work real hard,
The best you can do is render lard.

You wash real hard with lots of hope,
Get more results with a bar of soap.
By washin' gravel and shovelin' sand
You hope to get it in your hand.

It has been mined in former years,
A small nugget would give three cheers.
All we found that looked real bright
Was glittering sand and iron pyrite.

———◆———

*A psycho-ceramic is just another crackpot.*

# MARRIED LIFE

I love wimmen and married one,
Doing so was lots of fun.
She was skinny, but really sweet,
Loved her down to her big feet.

She cooked the beans and cornbread,
Swept the floor and made the bed.
Made a home a pleasant place,
She was sweet and no disgrace.

Every man should get a wife.
If you cultivate, have a good life.
Life is fun and for the birds,
But all along you will have words.

———◆———

*Asked my wife to sew up my shirt and it
seamed she would.*

# ALABAMA

Alabama, the loveliest state
Many think is less than great
They had the Wallaces, man and wife
Gave the state a pretty good life.

Many people thought they were smart
Stayin' in office is an Alabama art.
I have good taste and good expression,
But it was better than a depression.

I have to say the state has stills
Always find them back in the hills.
They've made and sold it for many a year.
Make poor whiskey and peddle beer.

You call the law and make complaint.
They make a raid, but the evidence ain't.
Folks are clean and won't have a bar,
But are willin' to lift a full fruit jar.

I lived in the state several years,
Political schemes reduce you to tears.
The law is written and seldom obeyed.
They think it's a game that's played.

Now I feel sorry for all those folks,
Live their lives with political jokes.
They take good care to check the polls,
But there's still dead people on the rolls.

# THE SEARCH

Huntin' for land is a lot of fun
If you have the gas to stay on the run,
From Tellico Plains upon the mountain
Like Ponce de Leon to find the fountain.

We looked all over those bloomin' hills
The price is higher than your winder sills.
I won't give up, but keep on lookin',
We need a place and not a rookin'.

The place I want ain't by a lake,
And I ain't scared of a rattlesnake.
It has to be a place on a stream.
It's the only way to fulfill a dream.

My wife agrees with what I need,
A heartfelt wish devoid of greed.
If our strength holds out we'll get it yet,
But are both unwillin' to make a bet.

# THE JUDGE

Fishing is a relaxing sport,
Ask the judge at the district court.
He owns a boat and trailer, too,
The most he ever caught was only a few.

He goes out early and comes in late,
Missed again his wife's dinner date.
She's up in the air eight hundred feet,
His tale of woe is about complete.

He made a promise to do some better,
She aims to test him to the letter.
The last trip out it seemed okay,
He didn't get home til the very next day.

The boat had to go, along with the trailer,
The judge now has a female jailer.
Now this sad tale ain't really so,
But be sure and tell her before you go.

# FISHIN'

Angling is the greatest sport,
My favorite pastime I can report.
Been to the mountains and fished in the
  sea,
And caught green trout with a black eyed
  pea.

The greatest fish I ever caught
Was with my shotgun and double aught.
Some would think it ain't all legal,
I pointed a bass with a neighbor's beagle.

I've been in the West and most of the East,
But a great big fish is a fascinating beast.
You see big trout and channel cat,
It's fun to fish wherever you're at.

Some folks say my tales are tall,
But look at the ones mounted on the wall.
I stop and admire them every day,
Since they're gone, they musta got away.

# FISH

Fish are creatures large and small
People catch and put on the wall.
Are found in water fresh and salt,
If you can't catch 'em, your own fault.

I've caught them big and caught them
   small,
But I ain't ever got one six feet tall.
To keep on tryin' is a must,
A real six-footer would make me bust.

I've caught some jacks and big green trout,
Sac au lait and chopique, but no horned
   pout,
Four kinds of catfish and lots of shad,
Now that kind of record ain't all bad.

Way out West we fished for trout,
Cutthroats and rainbows were all about,
Dolly Varden, brookies, a wary brown,
I've caught 'em all and iced 'em down.

Salmon are caught and mostly by hand,
I had a deft catch to grab the can.
Have caught others I will not mention,
Not on the creek, but by invention.

# MINNOWS

Minnows are a good fish food,
Now we fish 'em in the nude.
You can trap him with some bread,
Then the big fish can be fed.

If you drive up to Nantucket
Be sure and take a minnow bucket.
They are found North and South,
Get him in the basses mouth.

Can be purchased in a shop
Or at the river when you stop.
Get two dozen for your float,
Drop the bucket in the boat.

Now I fished a half a summer,
Without a minnow, would be dummer.
He's good for pike and walleye,
But for them he has to die.

I have fished over the land
And in China and Japan.
Never put him on a noose,
Extra ones we turn a loose.

# LAKE FISHIN'

We went fishin' on a lake,
In Ontario, for goodness sake.
There were islands all around,
Had our camp on solid ground.

Had a boat parked at the dock,
Also lots of granite rock.
Had to trap a fishin' minner,
Cause without them, got no dinner.

We caught pike and walleye, too,
Before we left was quite a few.
It was exciting, it was fine.
Up until I broke the line.

We stayed up for a week,
On the lake, was no creek.
It was great and it was neater,
If you ain't et by a skeeter.

# SUMMER FISHIN'

Have a son who is a drummer,
We both fish in spring and summer.
Talked it over, man to man,
And he wanted mountain land.

He came up just last week,
And we went out to the creek.
Hung his lure up in a tree,
Sure am glad it wasn't me.

We fished hard toward the lake,
And we ain't seen airy snake.
Fished on down to the truck,
Had some strikes, but no luck.

Fishin' hard in summer weather,
We had got it all together.
He went home a feelin' punk,
Ol man and boy had had a skunk.

# POSTED

Sit at home a feelin' dummer,
Ain't no place to fish this summer.
I went out one day last week,
They had posted all the creek.

Drove on out to another place,
Keep Out signs a real disgrace.
Thought that farmer was my friend,
But he wouldn't let us in.

Don't know where to go for trout,
Park the truck, but can't get out.
I went out the next day,
And I fished a pond for pay.

Now I like to fish the creek,
It's even good for the old and weak.
Now I don't know where to begin,
But I'll get caught if I sneak in.

# THE RIVER

Went to the river yesterday,
Floated all the entire way.
Trout were bitin' and jumpin' good,
That is better than cuttin' wood.

Caught two big 'uns in one pool,
Not so smart, but it was cool.
Strung 'em out behind the boat,
That's the way I like to float.

Got some more way on down.
Man, them trout were all around.
Didn't use a single minner,
He was willin' to eat my spinner.

She picked me up at five-thirty,
All tired out and plumb dirty.
She drug home a worn out guy,
But she had some fish to fry.

# SPINNER AND MINNER

Fishin' for trout I use a spinner,
When it gets slow I use a minner.
Have used worms and even flies,
But I found the fish too wise.

Wade the river and ride canoe,
That's the best I ever do.
My wife, she hauls me to the creek,
I'm goin' agin this comin' week.

Rainbow trout are in the water,
You are right, I went and caught 'er.
Throwed my lures a half a mile,
I'll get done in a little while.

———◆———

*Many poets are real wits, while others are just half of it.*

# CAMPIN'

I catch green trout in a boat,
We simply love to fish and float.
Don't go for gold, I ain't a fool,
Cannot stand cow pasture pool.

Can slowly float and make the scene,
Just the thing for an ex-marine.
Catch bream and bass all the way,
Fry 'em up and the end of the day.

Set up camp on a bluff,
Fishin' all day was enough.
The campfire was a pleasant sight,
Now it's time to say goodnight.

————◆————

*Found out a while back the Corps didn't
miss me at all. Didn't know 'til then that
mutual understanding could cause me so
much happiness.*

# CRICKETS

I take crickets to the creek,
Caught six trout just last week.
Run him on a little hook,
Mr. Rainbow can come and look.

When he takes I set the hook,
I catch trout by the book.
He may jump into the air,
Makes me glad to be there.

The cricket is a summer bait.
When fish is ready, is no wait.
For the cricket a raw deal,
Makes the fish a little meal.

You can buy 'em at the shop.
Goin' to the creek, make a stop
For fish bait the cricket's nice,
But he is just a sacrifice.

Bring the extra home with me,
Me and wifey like to see.
The lowly cricket cannot slurp,
But we like to hear him chirp.

# MY PASTIME

Fishing is a lot of fun,
You don't need a shotgun.
A cane pole cut on the creek
Can keep you busy about a week.

Float a boat or set on a bank,
Or in Texas, fish in a tank.
Have more fun wadin' the creek
If it were me I'd spend a week.

Have fished streams, rivers, and lakes,
I like 'em all for goodness sakes.
My wife done said to go and float,
But neither or us can find the boat.

———◆———

*Bill asked, "How's your wife gettin' along?"*
*I said, "I don't see how she could do any*
*better unless she took lockjaw."  Wimmen,*
*they're hard to understand.*

# GARDEN HACKLE

I have lots of fishin' tackle,
Also like my garden hackle.
Dig 'em up and watch 'em squirm,
It is just a lowly worm.

Attached to leader, hook, and rod
Fish are caught by any clod.
Floated thru a real deep pool,
Trout may hit just like a mule.

Set the hook when he takes,
You will like it, goodness sakes.
Now I have caught a lot of trout,
But I'm afraid not each time out.

———◆———

*After reviewing the book the critics made me
promise not to do it again.*

# ALABAMMER FISHING

I went fishin' in Alabammer,
Hit some catfish with a hammer.
Tried the same trick on a trout,
But I couldn't knock him out.

Then went out with a seine,
But it started a real bad rain.
Couldn't pull it by myself,
So I put it on the shelf.

Goin' home I met the law,
Didn't like what he saw.
Now he throwed me in the slammer,
For fishin' with a big claw hammer.

———◆———

*Got so dry in Texas one year some of the farmers had to use dehydrated water...a valuable resource as you only have to add five quarts to make a gallon.*

# HOOK AND BOBBER

Had a cane pole, hook, and bobber.
Stole it from another robber.
Dug a worm, put in a can.
Go and fish with the ol man.

Took a path to the creek,
Hadn't fished in half a week.
Dropped my hook behind a log,
Caught a turtle and my dog.

Cut the turtle right in two,
He would make a real good stew.
Now the mutt would only holler,
Would sell for less than half a dollar.

———◆———

*Me and Bill are retired brokers. You know,
two broker ol' boys you ain't likely to find.*

# LOW WATER

I went out to float the creek,
Hadn't been in over a week.
Weather was fine and water low.
Knew for sure it would be slow.

Had my bait and landing net,
Maybe I can catch him yet.
Throwed a lure on thru the pool,
But that trout was not a fool.

Then looked up and got a fly,
It's always good to give a try.
In a while I had a take,
So I fought him to the lake.


# ME AND BUDDY

I was goin' in a boat
If the bloomin' thing would float.
We had built it in the yard,
Way we did it wasn't hard.

Me and Buddy made the plan,
Talked it over man to man.
When we drug it to the creek,
All the thing would do was leak.

# THE U. P.

Gone to Michigan on the U.P.
We just had to go and see.
It has beauty, it is remote,
In the evening wear a coat.

We camped out on forest land,
Golden age passport in my hand.
We had driven quite a ways,
So we stayed for fifteen days.

Saw some deer and caught some trout.
We were glad we had come out.
Looked it over quite a lot,
But we needed the water hot.

Found a motel up near town,
We were glad to settle down.
Wife had thought she would croak,
But all she needed was a soak.

# BASSIN'

Bassin' way out on our lake,
Is lots of fun when they take.
Threw a bait and a plug,
Sometimes I use a bass bug.

Guess I am a fishin' sinner
When I reach down for a minner.
My choice for fishin' is my plugs,
Sometimes use fat June bugs.

Walked on in a lakeside thicket,
And reached for a little cricket.
Run him on a hook and line,
Then the fishin', it got fine.

But the fishin' it got slow,
Cause I couldn't get no mo'.
Went on home without a fish,
Still and all I sure can wish.

# UP NORTH

I went up North for my fishin'
All my life I had been wishin'.
We drove up in a truck,
Me and Maw, to try our luck.

We liked the country and the scenery,
But we couldn't find a beanery.
Cooked our grub beside the road,
She was willin' to help unload.

Drove the truck all the day,
And we got to Foleyet.
We checked in at the flyin' place,
But the cost was a real disgrace.

We flew out the next day,
Looking forward to our stay.
The cabin they had was a tent,
Now we wish we hadn't went.

# THE NORTH

I was raised up in the South,
Way up North was down in the mouth,
Country is pretty, the water clean,
The big ol pike are extra mean.

I went there to refresh my soul,
Even in summer it gets cold.
Took along my goose down jacket,
Hear the loons a makin' racket.

Lived on the lake about a week,
As much fun as the creek.
We flew out in the morning early,
Me and the pilot and my girlie.

———◆———

*Talked to the banker the other day about
banking some, but he didn't have much
interest in it.*

# ON THE BOAT

Fishin' the ocean is a lot of fun.
It can be done by anyone.
A piece of string to catch a crab,
Rod and reel for a small sand dab.

Go on the boat for an all day fee,
Get anything that swims in the sea.
Fish from the beach or on a pier,
It's easily done, have no fear.

You can go out early or come in late,
But don't go out without some bait.
You can toss a lure or even a tale,
But you will never catch a whale.

I used to go on the all day boat,
It's always a very exciting float.
Dropped our bait way down deep,
Found enough fish to make you weep.

# SMALLMOUTH

The smallmouth bass, a handsome fish,
You never catch with just a wish.
He's mostly found in a northern stream,
Catch a limit and your eye will gleam.

I've caught a few here in the South
And cooked enough to water your mouth.
I dress 'em out and get a skillet,
An expert hand with a big bass fillet.

Just like a trout, he's sure to jump.
A lot of fun, but hard on the pump.
You can wade the creek or take a float,
But wadin's more fun than in a boat.

A fly rod is the tool preferred,
A long back cast might catch a bird.
The ones I caught are mostly small,
Ain't got a one put on the wall.

You can go out early and come in late,
When ready to strike a real short wait.
A woman's not willin' to understand,
That chasin' a bass is good for a man.

# FLOATIN'

Boatin' the creek with my ol dog,
A lot more fun than shootin' a hog.
We throw our stuff in a 10 foot skiff,
Wife drops us off for a nice long drift.

Down the river and all of the creek.
We went three days, but could use a week.
I float and fish the whole day long,
Ol faithful dog just looks on.

We sleep at night beneath the stars,
Listen to owls, but never no cars.
We stretch a line across the river,
Catch turtles and cats with beef liver.

When we get home, we clean for a week,
Even faithful dog who's been in the creek.
My wife has said go do your thing,
A real small price to hear him sing.

Now floatin' the creek in a leaky boat,
The ideal thing for this ol goat.
Many men won't try or even consider
The relaxing days to be found on the river.

# WADIN'

I love to fish a whitewater creek,
The next time out I'll spend a week.
The red eye bass and native trout
Are mostly what it's all about.

When wadin' on down from pool to pool,
You slip on a rock and feel like a fool.
Bounce right up and make a cast,
You hope to hang a ten pound bass.

I fish all day and walk a mile,
And had such fun all the while.
Got home late and fried them all
Will keep a fishin' Spring til Fall.

———◆———

*Truth never hurt nobody.  Try it sometime.*

# FLY RODS

Wadin' the creek with a wonder rod,
Is good enough for a city clod.
A fly rod is the stick preferred,
A willow pole for a country bird.

Double taper line put on the stick
Will catch a trout both quick and slick.
A bamboo rod is a work of art,
After bein' in the creek, will come apart.

Grandpa used a rod of steel,
Had to save to get a reel.
Caught lots of trout on fly and bait,
Came on home, but was never late.

In this great age of fancy gear
Fly fish for trout and shoot at deer.
You catch a limit a fishin' a fly,
Don't really matter, wet or dry.

You spend hard money on a fancy pole.
It is a must to refresh your soul.
A wonder rod or split bamboo,
If you can save you might get two.

# CONSERVATION

Workin' the government, quite a job,
With the big boys we hob nob.
Went to work for the nation,
I was hired in conservation.

After college and degree
Had to work, no more whoopee.
Biology was my chosen field,
Now I had a seine to wield.

Filled fish ponds, cut the grass,
A custodian of great big bass.
Liked the work, the pay was small,
But we quit workin' in the Fall.

I raised trout and channel cat,
Fed them til they all got fat.
But twenty years of this life,
I had enough of government strife.

# SEMPER FIDELIS

The Marine Corps is a wonderful thing,
Hearing the song the recruiter sings.
Esprit de Corps and Semper Fi,
The good ol sergeant wouldn't lie.

I went in at seventeen,
A skinny kid, both lean and green.
Boot camp whipped us up in style.
We hit the grinder mile on mile.

Across the ocean and into war,
Jungle livin' over thar.
We came on leave in '44,
But went back to fight some more.

When it was over I got out,
But in a year there was a doubt.
Went back in to go for twenty,
Spit and polish and drill a plenty

Traveled the Corps and saw the boys,
And as a sergeant I made noise.
I took a wife and a little leave,
Did my duty and didn't grieve.

Across the ocean and all around,
Coast to coast and up and down.
We went on orders where they sent,
Still there's places we ain't went.

Time ran out, I got some age,
Took my pension as honest wage.
The dear old Corps, they cannot stir,
Cause I don't have to transfer.


# AT SEA

I have floated on the sea,
Made me weak in the knee.
A smooth sail is like devotion,
But what gets me is the motion.

I have seen it really rough,
Don't take long to get enough.
Can tell you what it's all about,
Liable to turn you inside out.

# THE OCCUPATION

Spent many years in the Corps,
Had enough, don't need no more.
Didn't think my mind was twisted,
But to tell the truth, I enlisted.

They sent us to the western coast,
Can tell you how we drilled the most.
We only drilled when it was dry,
Sure did have a good D. I.

I look back over the years,
Post to post and many cold beers.
Put us on a Navy ship,
Had to go and fight the Nip.

I came back home in '44,
After leave, I went some more.
Stood on a ship watchin' the land
I was goin' to Japan.

We had set the Rising Sun,
But our work had just begun.
Slant-eyed girls and spit-toed shoes
That is history; it ain't news.

# THE OCEAN

I don't like a lot of motion,
So I went and left the ocean.
Sailin' ships some say are fine,
To tell the truth, they aren't mine.

In the Pacific, the North Atlantic,
Tell you now them seas were frantic.
On a big ship we put out,
From the first I had my doubt.

We sailed on for many a day,
Finally landed in Norway.
Oslo was the place we found,
So we stopped and looked around.

We got to stay a night and day
Then we up and sailed away.
Now that trip wasn't a lark,
Next we landed in Denmark.

Told the story of my sailin'
And by now my belly's ailin',
It was good for me I guess,
But I am sailin' less and less.

# RETIREMENT

Have been to China and Japan,
But I retired to mountain land.
Like it great up in the hills,
Am willin' to hear the whip-poor-wills.

Mine has beauty; it is remote,
Never see a billy goat.
Trees and rocks and runnin' water,
Has been seen by son and daughter.

Got ten acres on a stream,
The answer to a lifetime dream.
Wife don't like it - we ain't fussed,
Better than that, she hasn't cussed.

———◆———

*The Corps said they were gonna send me to*
*OCS...and they did– over choppy seas.*

# THE CORPS

The dear ol Corps I do not miss,
Said goodbye without a kiss.
When I went and drove away
It sure gave me a real good day.

For twenty years we played the game.
Spit and polish was the name.
Drill the troops 'til we got sore
Get up next day for even more.

We went to sea on a Navy ship,
Usually a tiring, boring trip.
Navy beans and sweet cornbread,
The perfect meal to sicken the dead.

Time went by from post to post.
Parris Island we hated the most.
But time ran out; we went away.
Am a civil servant on half-pay.

———◆———

*As they say in the Corps, "You can tell a
second lieutenant, but you can't tell him
much."*

# TRAVELIN'

I have traveled thru the land,
Then to China and Japan.
I am old and partly bent,
But I like the Orient.

Many men in our world
Brought them home a slant-eyed girl.
My folks told me to be wise,
I am hooked on our round eyes.

Went on thru the southern seas,
Didn't like it, if you please.
Coconut palms and dusky eyes,
Give it to the other guys.

I got home among the last,
Guv'ment travelin', it ain't fast.
Now I don't care about the boat.
Had way too much time afloat.

# MILITARY LIFE

I am old; I am contrary–
Learned it in the military.
Twenty years of movin' around,
I have seen a lot of ground.

Military life is called tough,
Don't take long to get enough.
Boys come in and stay a time
Soon will seek another clime.

I have seen many men
Come to know the fix he's in.
The life is borin' and it's hard,
Then they put him walkin' guard.

I went in and did my time
Thought I would be caught in crime.
Did it all; I didn't quit.
Tell you boys I'm out of it.

# THE PROMISE

Jimmy is a smilin' man,
This ol boy just ain't his fan.
I'm willin' to listen to them talk
I've also heard a parrot squawk.

He said some things to get elected,
No sooner in than he defected...
Energy crisis, employment needs,
Help for farmers, and government seeds.

The man has said, "I'll handle things,"
But we ain't likin' what he brings.
A promise made, he cannot keep.
It will soon make a nation weep.

A few more years he'll run again,
But we will have enough by then.
I urge you now to stop and think
If he don't get busy we will sink.

# THE PARTY

Political parties are okay,
If you don't care what they say.
Say too little of the facts,
In both the second and third acts.

We hear the promise and the speech,
As many as an owl could screech.
We listen close on the TV,
Lied again to you and me.

We must bear up and endure,
Go to the polls that's for sure.
Many candidates have defected,
Now look and see what we elected.

———◆———

*A hunnerd years from now the comedy
writers will never want for material. They
will have our Congressional Record.*

# PHIL AND BOB

Phil Gramm and Bobby Dole
Promise to make the country whole.
We will listen to the tube,
Will be as slick as jiffy lube.

Votin' season is at hand,
Much hot air in the land.
We don't really want no more,
Cause we heard it all before.

Go to the polls with my wife.
We hope they get 10 years to life.
Now I have went and had my say,
Please be ready for election day.


# THE POLLS

Went to the polls to make a choice,
We had heard a republican voice.
Loud and clear it had a ring,
Made a promise for everything.

We had heard it many times
Probably committed several crimes.
I know I'm old and gettin' fat,
So please elect a democrat.

# ARKANSAS

This whole nation's in a mess
When Billy Clinton changed address.
He started out in Arkansas,
Hard to believe what we saw.

Little Rock came to Washington
With an Arkansas favorite son.
Some looked on fearful bad
Cause we knew we had been had.

We have read of the necropolis,
But he gave us Stephanopoulos.
Brought him in as his adviser,
As much sense as warm budweiser.

A capitol gang he put in place,
Set us up a real rat race.
All of this and Billary,
Can do no good to this country.

# B & H

Here's to Bill and Hillary,
Makes us wonder, you and me.
Ain't a credit to the South,
Way out West would be a drouth.

We never thought he'd be elected,
Political payback was collected.
He got in and brought his wife,
Ain't no help, just plain strife.

Four full years were given away,
Still supports the lez and gay.
You and I have seen it all,
Get rid of them in the Fall.

———◆———

*The man we got in office is a long way from
being precedent of the United States.*

# MAN'S BEST FRIEND

Man's best friend is just a dog.
He'll love you in rain, snow, or fog.
Many folks don't understand
Why a mutt is a must for a man.

A dog is willin' to help you hunt,
Also to growl, bark, and grunt.
Many say a real bad habit,
Not when you need to run a rabbit.

Are many breeds and different sizes,
But with mutts I sympathizes.
Low down dogs, near the ground,
Sometimes hard to get around.

Had a friend who was a vet
And he had a dog to pet.
Now he said, "That mutt is wise,
Go and look into his eyes."

Waggin tail and pleading eyes,
It is a fact and no disguise.
I have had a number of dogs,
Never cut wood or drag logs.

When the last one died, we were hurt.
We felt lower than fill dirt.
It ain't a matter of our pride,
Hurt us when the ol dog died.

# WALKING

I took my friend on a nice long hike,
Forest Service sign said No Motor Bike.
We got up real early and packed our gear.
Wives watched us go with a great deal of
    fear.

We drove up the mountain, way to the
    top.
Up through the clouds, a terrible drop.
We parked the car at the start of the trail.
We felt extra good and could not fail.

A way down the river and on through the
    trees,
We forded the river up to our knees.
We walked and we waded and looked for a
    spot.
We both had our lunch, we hadn't forgot.

A nice feeder brook by a large trout
    stream.
We both had found it, it wasn't a dream.
After pitching our tents we fished two
    days,
And walked down the river an awful
    ways.

The casting was excellent, the fly rod great,
But couldn't get a fish with no kind of
    bait.
My friend fished hard and caught one
    small,
It's a verified fact, the tale ain't tall.

We quit the river and checked the small
    streams.
We couldn't catch fish, it was no dream.
We explored the creeks and one of the
    falls.
He lost his footing and near broke it all.

We got up real early the very next day,
And packed our stuff without delay.
Puffed down the trail and over the top,
Kept right on walking, but very near
    dropped.

We had to stop for a small lunch break,
By a trailside stream, there wasn't a lake.
On up to the top we found his car,
A lot more welcome than a big camp fire.

———◆———

*Man over in Arkansas several years ago said
to me, "Have you seen any of them walkin'
catfish?" Only thing I could tell him was I'd
seen two of them hitchhiking through
Jackson, Mississipi, one day.*

# JOHNS

John and John are boys of note
Now all they learned was got by rote.
They love to hunt and catch a fish,
Could go ever day if they had their wish.

To camp in the woods is their delight
They can set up camp and seldom fight.
These two boys, they are the best,
Can pass anything but an English test.

Can shoot at squirrels high in a tree,
They might hit one by age twenty-three.
I know this shootin', it ain't the best.
In fact, he only hit the nest.

Cookin' is somethin' they both enjoy,
You can't really fill up either boy.
The old man's taters real well fried
Are put away with lots of pride.

Biscuits and gravy are allright, too,
When they get done it's more than a few.
Corn bread and beans are called coarse
    fare,
But they can take care of 'em anywhere.

It's about time to stop this tale,
Get the skillet and fry the quail.
These boys I miss and I must say,
I'd like to see 'em ever day.

# THE TROOP

Out in the woods with 18 boys,
Pitched their tents and made some noise.
Came in the truck with the trailer in back
And all their grub in a brown paper sack.

With three patrols in several tents,
Would make fires if they found their flints.
The food was cooked and eaten soon,
Washed greasy dishes by the light of the
    moon.

When cleanin' up they can't get goin',
A good bit like the front yard mowin'.
I make loud threats and offer advice,
But to get it done it may take twice.

They went to bed just after nine
Talkin' still and feelin' fine.
I woke 'em up at the morning sun
To gather wood and have more fun.

I have camped out with several groups,
But had more fun with a Boy Scout
    Troop.
To any man who's willin' to give
Go teach a boy the clean way to live.

# TEACHIN'

Trainin' boys is where it's at,
Short or tall or even fat.
We take them all outside to camp,
It doesn't matter, dry or damp.

To make a fire they split the wood,
Steel and flint was no good.
They keep a tryin', is a must,
But this requirement is a bust.

They work hard around the tent,
Jaws a flappin', their backs are bent.
Tents are tight, the lanterns lit,
Went inside in a little bit.

Sleepin' bags laid on the ground
Inside the tent away from town.
Talked it over half the night,
But they get up at first light.

# THE CAMP

The Boy Scout camp is a lonesome place,
Without the boys, a real disgrace.
On Monday morning just after camp
It's mostly deserted, desolate and damp.

On Friday night they came in troops,
Both men and boys, an impressive group.
They pitched some tents and cut some
        wood,
Cooked a lot, but nothin' good.

They went to bed and slept the night,
Had some words, but never a fight.
After gettin' up late for ham and eggs,
Filled them up, including both legs.

An all day romp at scoutin' around,
Went to the campfire and sat on the
        ground.
They had their awards and sang a song.
It was all over before too long.

Got up early and folded their tents,
Up the trail and away they went.
They will come back another day
To the Boy Scout camp not far away.

# TV WATCHIN'

I sat down to watch TV,
Little decent to stop and see.
Many people laugh and scoff,
But they will not turn it off.

The weather channel and CNN,
That's a safe place to begin.
Outdoor channel came on line,
Showed us fishin' extra fine.

Wholesome programs hard to find,
Gotta have somethin' to unwind.
If you look and carefully choose
There is always the evening news.

If it's dull and don't excite
Turn the channel and see the fight.
Have a channel for all sports,
None at all for book reports.

Much of it is unclean,
Shootin' folks and extra mean.
Even in an hour show
See the sex and say, "Oh, no."

Hard to find a decent slot
In spite of all they have got.
Don't get mad and gripe and scoff,
Why not stop and turn it off.

# EASY LIVIN'

Now I lived in Arkansas,
And we liked what we saw.
They have turkey, quail, and trout,
And beautiful scenery all about.

Friendly people and Southern ways,
That's the way I spend my days.
You don't have to rush and scurry,
Southern folks ain't in a hurry.

Lazy days and easy livin',
Without a job, it is forgiven.
Have our garden and some cows,
Also feedin' two ol sows.

That's the life we came to enjoy,
Just the thing for this ol boy.
Time ran out, we went away.
Sure am sorry I couldn't stay.

# AT CHURCH

Went to church the other day,
This is what I heard him say.
Sin will get you into Hell,
Are never saved by any bell.

You must believe; you must obey,
Or be lost in the final day.
That day is comin' sometime soon,
Could be April, May, or June.

Don't live a life of constant fear,
But be ready for Him to appear.
I have believed for many years
In spite of weakness, toil, and tears.

Obeyin' the scriptures and command,
Will get you to the promised land.
Some won't make it in that day
They had chosen the evil way.

# IN TENNESSEE

Up in the mountains of Tennessee,
Beautiful place to go and see.
I have hunted and fished therein,
Also with my son and friend.

Mountain men are debonair,
Whatever you do, they don't care.
They are cool and quite remote
And the good book they can quote.

Love the mountains and it's folks,
Sometimes stop and tell them jokes.
Most are good and honest men,
And he makes a trusted friend.

---◆---

*Told the candidate at the meeting last night,
"I know what you're gonna speak on." He
said, "What?" I answered, "On and on and
on and on..."*

# THE WAR

Civil War still bein' fought,
But it's really done for nought.
Now my folks were in the fight,
Had to run both day and night.

Middle brother helped the South,
In wet or dry or even drouth.
Were two more on the other side,
One was calvary and got to ride.

Little brother was alerted,
In mid-summer, he deserted,
But came back and turned in,
Knew desertion was a sin.

They mustered out in Arkansas,
North had won, it warn't a draw.
This here story's old and sad,
But was related by Grandad.

# SIN

Sittin' in the house thinkin' of sin
And the awful fix I'm in.
Thought I would go out and steal,
There was no one who would squeal.

It came to me that it was wrong,
But I knew it all along.
I had heard the preacher say
Sin will send the other way.

Come this Sunday goin' to service,
I know it's goin' to make me nervous.
I ain't sick and will not fight,
Think it's time to get it right.

———◆———

*The old preacher said the man he talked to
wanted to come into the church, but he
couldn't since there were so many hypocrites
in it. Preacher said, "That's quite allright,
there's always room for one more."*

# ALL ALONG

I write a poem all along
And can tell you right from wrong.
The world today is full of sin,
It is seen by faithful men.

Have read the scriptures, know it's true.
It has meaning for me and you.
One laid claim to returning from dead,
But that ain't what the Good Book said.

The scripture was given long ago,
By faith we know it all is so.
Now don't get scared and have a fright,
We live by faith and not by sight.

God has given His command
Must be obeyed by mortal man.
He loves us all and gave His Son,
We also have a race to run.

# ROUGH TIMES

I have writ it kind of hard,
Of dogs, and wimmen, and renderin' lard,
Turnip greens and pot likker,
It is on the ol man's slicker.

Times were rough in the South,
We had little for our mouth.
Many worked hard behind the mule,
All considered, it was cool.

Many had an old milk cow,
Cannot hook 'er to the plow.
If you can't plow, will get weak,
Now that is really up the creek.

———◆———

*Since my wife is a wise ol woman, does that
make her a sage hen?*

117

# THE PRINTER

Went to the printer with my verse,
And he said, "I've never seen worse."
Wasn't sure that I could write,
And it wasn't done for spite.

He set it on the linotype
Cause it was really gettin' ripe.
It was printed, it was bound,
Now the author can't be found.

We sent the book for review,
Critic said, "I hope you're through."
I had had a lot of hope,
Printer said, "Go use a rope."

❖

*Lighter side of life is great– please don't you be overweight.*

# VERSES

Sit in the house writin' verse,
My wife said put in the hearse.
I have writ of dogs and men,
It ain't hard when I begin.

When you read what I wrote
You will figger I missed the boat.
Now I don't think that I am dumb,
Still I have to go write some.

My verse is short, the message sweet,
But it is never incomplete.
I like to write it in the night,
But never work til broad daylight.

Have writ stories of cuttin' logs,
And my threat to drag the dogs.
If you think the story tough,
This may well be quite enough.

# SO LONG

We have come to the end of the book,
I am glad you could take a look.
Worked on it for several years,
Hope you laugh and have no tears.

I know the verse is not the best,
Most of it is given in jest.
Told you what I mostly do,
Just like me, it isn't new.

Started writing years ago,
As I age, I surely get slow.
Hope you think that some are funny,
But it wasn't done for money.

I think the tale is overlong,
Even with a fiddle song.
Will have to stop and put it away,
You guessed it right, I called it a day.

To order additional copies of *Poetic Injustice*, complete the information below.

Ship to: (please print)

Name_____

Address_____

City, State, Zip_____

_____ copies of *Poetic Injustice* @ $11.95 each  $ _____
Postage and handling @$2.50 per book  $ _____
Georgia residents add 6% tax  $ _____
Total Amount Enclosed  $ _____

*Make checks payable to* **Fireside Publishing**
**Send to: George Statham**
**P.O. Box 282 • Hiawassee, GA 30546**

--------------------------------------------------------------------------------

To order additional copies of *Poetic Injustice*, complete the information below.

Ship to: (please print)

Name_____

Address_____

City, State, Zip_____

_____ copies of *Poetic Injustice* @ $11.95 each  $ _____
Postage and handling @$2.50 per book  $ _____
Georgia residents add 6% tax  $ _____
Total Amount Enclosed  $ _____

*Make checks payable to* **Fireside Publishing**
**Send to: George Statham**